ANNAPOLIS VALLEY TASTES

Recipes from the Valley's Best Restaurants

with Sean Buckland

Photographs by

Colleen Dagnall and Bob Federer

NIMBUS
PUBLISHING

Nimbus Publishing Limited
PO Box 9166, Halifax, NS B3K 5M8
(902) 455-4286 www.nimbus.ca

Printed and bound in Canada

Design: Kate Westphal, Graphic Detail Inc., Charlottetown, PE
Sean Buckland photo: Colleen Dagnall
Colleen Dagnall and Bob Federer photo: Tracy Southey

Library and Archives Canada Cataloguing in Publication

Buckland, Sean, 1976-
Annapolis Valley tastes : recipes from the valley's best restaurants / Sean Buckland.
Includes index.
ISBN 978-1-55109-703-9

1. Cookery—Nova Scotia—Annapolis Valley. 2. Restaurants—Nova Scotia—Annapolis Valley. I. Title.
TX715.6.B794 2009 641.59716'3 C2008-907036-4

We acknowledge the financial support of the Government of Canada through the Book Publishing Industry Development Program (BPIDP) and the Canada Council, and of the Province of Nova Scotia through the Department of Tourism, Culture and Heritage for our publishing activities.

table of contents

introduction

The Annapolis Valley is known for the rolling farmlands that hug its coastline, rest on its mountain slopes, and lay on its floor. The Valley is nestled between the North and South mountains that run parallel to Nova Scotia's Fundy shore, an ideal setting for both fishing and agriculture. The Valley's sheltered location along the coast helps to moderate its temperatures in the winter and concentrate its heat in the summer, giving it the perfect climate for farming a wide variety of fruit and vegetable crops—from summer berries and tomatoes to fall pumpkins and, of course, apples.

I can remember piling into the back seat of the family station wagon every fall as a young boy and heading for the Valley to fill our buckets full of delicious Gravenstein and Cortland apples. Now that station wagon is a sedan and I find myself in the driver's seat, heading to the Valley to dine at the incredible restaurants that call the region home.

From Windsor in the east to Clare in the west, a great number of restaurants in the Valley are operated by artisan chefs determined upon using only the freshest local ingredients. With fresh seafood, meat, and produce available year-round, the Valley provides inspiration for seasonal menu selections that offer an entirely new culinary experience each time you visit. The snow peas and grape tomatoes harvested at the end of July make for a wonderful accompaniment to any main dish. The strawberries and raspberries harvested toward the end of summer create fabulous desserts that Nova Scotians look forward to all year round. The variety of squashes harvested in the fall make excellent comfort soups to keep you warm when the cold weather arrives.

For food enthusiasts or at-home chefs, a trip to one of the local farmers' markets in the Valley is an experience in itself—it's easy to get lost in sorting through bins of fresh corn, choosing from the many varieties of apples, or waiting patiently for fresh bread to come out of the oven. If you are anything like me, you won't have a clue what you are going to prepare for dinner when you visit the farmers' market; instead, you will let yourself be led by what has been brought in fresh by the local farmers.

Where there is great food, great wine follows, and the Valley is no exception to the rule. As a food enthusiast, I always insist on pairing the local wine with the local food. There are several award-winning vineyards in the Valley producing a variety of exceptional vintages—from Blomidon Estate Winery's L'Acadie Blanc to Saint-Familles Wines's Marechal Foch to the fabulous dessert wines from Domaine de Grand Pré, Gaspereau Vineyards, and L'Acadie Vineyards—so it's always easy to find the perfect local wine to accompany a dinner made from fresh Valley produce.

The recipes in this book are about combining the finest local chefs with the freshest local foods to experience the true taste of the Annapolis Valley. Whether you are donning your chef aprons and preparing a bowl of Valley Corn Chowder with Smokey Bacon, baking Peach-Blueberry Crumble Pie for a family get-together, or dining at Tempest Restaurant to experience chef Michael Howell's Dijon, Hazelnut, and Parmesan Crusted Lamb Racks, the recipes in this book are sure to bring the Valley to you and you to the Valley!

Bon appétit!

soups and starters

A wide range of seasonal Annapolis Valley fruits and vegetables are readily available at any time of the year, and this fresh produce is a perfect base for locally inspired appetizers, from crisp salads to hearty chilies and chowders. Whether you are taking advantage of the raspberry harvest in July or the pumpkin harvest in the middle of September, the possibilities to create soups and starters that are sure to tantalize your taste buds are endless.

facing page: The Lookoff

ground beef soup

Makes 12 to 14 servings (about 4 quarts).

2 tablespoons butter
2 pounds lean ground beef
2 cups chopped Spanish onion
2 cloves garlic, chopped
1 1/2 cups sliced carrots
1 cup snapped green or yellow beans
2 cups chopped celery
1 cup diced green peppers
1 cup diced red peppers
12 cups (3 quarts) beef broth
1 cup chopped fresh tomato
1/4 teaspoon ground black pepper
Fresh parsley for garnish (optional)

Melt the butter in a six-quart saucepan. Add the ground beef and cook on medium heat, stirring often, until the beef has browned. Add the onion, garlic, carrots, beans, celery, and green and red peppers, and stir. Cover and let simmer on low heat for 15 minutes. Stir the beef broth into the saucepan. Add the tomato and black pepper and stir. Cover and let simmer on low heat for 55 minutes, stirring occasionally.

To serve, ladle the soup into bowls and garnish each serving with fresh parsley.

Falcourt Inn
Nictaux

Middleton

cold raspberry soup with white chocolate mousse and lemon-infused yogourt

Makes 15 servings.

Raspberry Soup

2 cups plus 1 teaspoon cranberry juice, divided
1/2 cup dry white wine
1 sprig of mint (left whole)
1 large orange (zest and juice)
1 vanilla bean, scraped
18 ounces (about 4 cups) raspberries
Sugar to taste
1 1/2 teaspoons cornstarch

In a large saucepan over medium heat, combine 2 cups of the cranberry juice with the white wine, mint, orange zest and juice, and vanilla bean. Add the raspberries and simmer until the raspberries are a soft mush. Strain the mixture, reserving only the liquid. Continue cooking the liquid on low heat until it starts to bubble.

Sweeten the soup to taste, adding a bit of sugar at a time until it reaches your preferred sweetness. In a small bowl, stir the cornstarch and the remaining teaspoon of cranberry juice together until the cornstarch is smooth and free of lumps. Add the cornstarch mixture to the soup sparingly to thicken it lightly (when finished, it should resemble a medium-thick broth). Remove the soup from heat and let it stand at room temperature to cool for 30 to 40 minutes before serving.

White Chocolate Mousse

9 ounces white chocolate
2 teaspoons 35% whipping cream (heavy cream)
1 whole egg
1 egg yolk
2 sheets (2 1/2 x 8 1/2) gelatin (do not use powdered gelatin)
2 1/4 cups 35% whipping cream (heavy cream), whipped

Place the white chocolate in the top of a double boiler. (If a double boiler isn't available, fill a large saucepot partway with water and bring to a boil. Reduce heat to low and simmer. Place a medium-sized mixing bowl overtop of the water, making sure that the bottom of the bowl does not touch the water. Place the white chocolate in the bowl.) Add the 2 teaspoons of unwhipped cream to the chocolate and cook, stirring often, until the chocolate has melted. Do not overheat the chocolate or it will separate.

Soak the gelatin sheets in ice water for 5 minutes. Meanwhile, in a second double boiler or bowl atop saucepan, whisk together the egg and egg yolk. Once the gelatin sheets are finished soaking, remove them from the water and squeeze them to get rid of the excess water. Stir the gelatin sheets into the egg mixture in the top of the double boiler. Pour the melted chocolate into the egg mixture and stir. Remove from heat and allow the mixture to cool.

When the mixture is cool to the touch, fold in the whipped cream. Place the mousse in the refrigerator to set. (Ideally, the mousse should be left to set overnight.)

Lemon Yogourt

1 lemon (zest and juice)
1 cup plain yogourt
Sugar to taste

Warm the lemon juice in a small saucepan over low heat. Add the zest and stir for about a minute, or until the zest has softened. Remove the lemon mixture from the heat and allow it to cool to room temperature. Once it has cooled, stir the lemon mixture into the yogourt. Sweeten the yogourt sparingly with sugar to taste.

To serve, ladle the soup into soup plates, place a dollop of the mousse on top, and drizzle with the yogourt.

Acton's Grill & Café
Wolfville

chicken caesar salad with sautéed apples and cashews

Makes 4 servings.

Caesar Salad Dressing

4 or 5 whole garlic cloves, peeled
1 teaspoon salt
1/4 teaspoon coarse black pepper
1/4 cup lemon juice
1/2 teaspoon Dijon mustard
2 eggs
1 1/2 cups vegetable oil

In a food processor, purée the peeled garlic cloves with the salt, pepper, lemon juice, and Dijon mustard. Add the eggs and blend. With the food processor running, slowly drizzle the vegetable oil into the mix. (If the dressing separates, it is usually possible to save it by mixing in another egg and 1/4 teaspoon of Dijon mustard.)

Wolfville

Salad

1 large head of romaine lettuce
6–7 tablespoons Caesar salad dressing, divided (see recipe, left)
1/2 cup herbed croutons
3/4 cup shaved Parmesan cheese
3/4 cup grated mozzarella cheese
4 large chicken breasts, roasted
3 large unpeeled cooking apples, cut into 1/2-inch slices (Gravenstein or Cortland are best)
1/2 cup unsalted whole cashew nuts

Wash and dry the leaves of the romaine lettuce, then tear them into bite-sized pieces and place them in a large bowl. Toss in 2 to 3 tablespoons of the Caesar salad dressing 1 tablespoon at a time until the salad is dressed to your preference. Add the croutons, Parmesan cheese, and mozzarella cheese, and toss the salad again. Distribute onto small salad plates and set aside.

Slice the roasted chicken breasts into bite-sized wedges. Place 4 tablespoons of the Caesar salad dressing into a medium-sized frying pan on medium-high heat. Add the chicken pieces, apple slices, and cashews. Stir gently every few seconds for approximately three minutes. Do not overcook; the apples should not be allowed to soften.

Top each salad with an equal portion of the chicken, apple, and cashew mixture. If desired, garnish each plate with Parmesan shavings, grated mozzarella, and croutons.

The Ivy Deck Garden Bistro
Wolfville

hiibaleipa rye bread with spiced crabapple jelly

Makes approximately 7 cups or 7 (8-ounce) jars of jelly and 6 servings (two loaves) of bread.

Spiced Crabapple Jelly

1 bushel (about 8 1/2 quarts) fresh crabapples
1 (57 gram) package fruit pectin crystals
1/2 teaspoon cinnamon
Pinch of cloves
4 1/2 cups granulated sugar

Wash the crabapples and cut them into 1-inch pieces without peeling or coring them. Place the crabapple pieces in a large stockpot with enough water to cover the fruit, and cook covered on medium-high heat until the crabapples are mushy. Strain the fruit through a cheesecloth, reserving the juice only, and making sure not to stir or press the pulp while it is in the cloth, as this will cloud the jelly.

In a 4- or 8-quart stockpot, combine 4 cups of the crabapple juice with the fruit pectin crystals, cinnamon, and cloves. Place over high heat, stirring constantly until the mixture comes to a hard boil. Reduce the heat slightly and continue boiling for 2 minutes.

Add the sugar all at once, stir, and bring the mixture to a full rolling boil for 2 more minutes, stirring often. Remove the jelly mixture from the heat, skim off any foam that may have accumulated, and place the jelly in hot sterile jars. Seal the jars tightly with lids.

Hiibaleipa Rye Bread

2 tablespoons butter or shortening
1 tablespoon granulated sugar
2 teaspoons salt
1 1/2 cups hot water
1/2 cup warm water
1 (8 gram) package active dry yeast
3 cups rye flour
2–3 cups all-purpose flour

Combine the butter or shortening, sugar, salt, and hot water in a large mixing bowl and let the mixture stand until lukewarm. Pour the warm water in a separate small bowl and sprinkle the yeast overtop, taking care not to stir the yeast into the water. Allow the yeast to set in the warm water for 5 minutes, or until the surface is covered in small lumps.

Once the yeast has set, pour the yeast mixture into the large bowl and stir. Mix in the rye flour and beat for 10 minutes using dough hooks, beaters, or wooden spoons.

Stir small amounts of all-purpose flour into the dough mixture until it is elastic (usually 2 to 2 1/2 cups of flour). Knead the dough 10 minutes by hand, then place it in a greased bowl and let it rise for 1 hour.

Punch down the raised dough, then split it into two balls and press each ball into a 1-inch-thick circle. Place the dough circles on a greased cookie sheet and let them rise for about 1 hour, or until they have doubled in size. Do not let them rise for too long, or the bread will have large holes.

Bake the dough at 400°F for 25 to 30 minutes, or until the bread has browned to a medium darkness.

Cut the bread into wedges and serve hot with butter and spiced crabapple jelly.

Note: For whole wheat bread, substitute 3 cups of whole wheat flour for the 3 cups of rye flour.

The Tin Pan Bakery & Bistro
Port Williams

Digby

lobster bisque

Makes 4 servings.

4 small cooked lobsters
1 tablespoon butter
1 tablespoon canola oil
2 medium yellow onions, diced small
4 stalks celery, diced
2 large carrots, diced small
2/3 cup tomato paste
1 unpeeled bulb garlic, sliced in half horizontally
2 bay leaves
1 tablespoon peppercorns
4 tablespoons brandy
1 cup white wine
1/3 cup all-purpose flour
1 3/4 quarts low-sodium chicken stock
3/4 cup 10% half-and-half cream (blend cream)
Sea salt to taste
Pepper to taste

Remove the meat and stomachs from the lobsters and discard the stomachs. Retain the shells for use in the bisque. Slice the meat into bite-sized pieces, then set it aside. Cut the body shells into quarters and break the other remaining shells into small pieces.

Place the butter and oil in a large stockpot and cook over medium-high heat until the butter melts. Add the onion, celery, and carrot and cook, stirring often, for about 15 minutes, or until the vegetables are caramelized. Stir in the tomato paste and cook for 12 minutes, stirring often. Add the lobster shells, garlic, bay leaves, and peppercorns. Cook for 3 minutes, stirring constantly. Add the brandy and white wine, stirring constantly until the liquid has reduced by half. Sprinkle the flour into the pot and stir well for 2 minutes. Slowly add the chicken stock, stirring until the mixture is free of lumps. Simmer the bisque uncovered on low heat for 90 minutes, stirring occasionally.

Strain the bisque, reserving only the liquid. Pour the liquid into a medium-sized saucepan and stir in the cream. Place the saucepan on medium-low heat and simmer until the liquid reaches 160°F, taking care not to let the bisque boil. Add sea salt and pepper to taste.

To serve, divide the lobster meat into four equal portions and place each portion on the bottom of a soup plate. Spoon the bisque overtop of the meat.

Halls Harbour Lobster Pound
Halls Harbour

Halls Harbour

mussels with double-smoked bacon and vermouth

Makes 2 servings.

1/4 pound salted butter, softened
Pinch fresh parsley
1/4 cup puréed garlic
1 tablespoon white wine
1 drop hot pepper sauce
1 drop Worcestershire sauce
1/2 tablespoon lemon juice
Pinch cracked black pepper
1/4 cup diced red onion
1/4 cup chopped double-smoked bacon, in medium-sized pieces
1 1/2 pounds mussels
3 tablespoons sweet vermouth
2 lemon wedges for garnish (optional)

Place the butter, parsley, garlic, white wine, hot pepper sauce, Worcestershire sauce, lemon juice, and cracked black pepper in a large pot over medium high heat. Stir the mixture constantly until the butter melts.

Once the butter has melted, add the red onion and sauté for 2 to 3 minutes, or until the onion appears translucent. Stir in the bacon and mussels, then the vermouth. Cover and steam over high heat until the mussels open (about 5 minutes).

To serve, divide the mussels between two large soup bowls and garnish each serving with a lemon wedge.

Blomidon Inn
Wolfville

Cape Blomidon

porter cheddar soup

Makes 10 to 12 servings.

3 tablespoons butter
1 large white onion, chopped
1 celery stalk, chopped
2 medium carrots, peeled and chopped
3 tablespoons all-purpose flour
2 cups vegetable broth
2 medium potatoes, peeled and cubed
1 roasted red pepper, peeled and chopped
2 cups porter or other dark beer
2 cups 35% whipping cream (heavy cream)
Grated nutmeg to taste
1/8 teaspoon cayenne pepper
Salt to taste
3 cups old cheddar cheese, shredded
1 cup imperial sharp cheddar cheese
Additional shredded cheddar cheese or diced roasted red peppers for garnish (optional)

Melt the butter in a large pot. Add the onion, celery, and carrots, and cook uncovered over medium heat until soft (about five minutes). Sift the flour in slowly and cook for one minute, stirring often. Mix in the broth, then add the potatoes, roasted red pepper, and beer. Bring to a boil, then reduce heat to low, cover, and simmer for 20 minutes, or until the potatoes are soft.

Remove the vegetables from the pot using a large slotted spoon and transfer them to a food processor or blender. Blend until puréed. Return the vegetable purée to the pot, then add the cream, nutmeg, cayenne, and salt to taste. Whisk thoroughly until combined. Reheat over medium heat until the liquid comes to a simmer. Add the imperial and old cheddar cheeses 1/2 cup at a time and stir until melted, taking care not to let the mixture boil.

Serve hot, garnished with additional shredded cheddar cheese and/or diced roasted red pepper.

The Port Pub and Bistro
Port Williams

Port Williams

pumpkin chili

Makes 4 to 6 servings.

1 tablespoon cooking oil
1 large white onion, diced
1 tablespoon cumin seed
1 tablespoon smoked paprika
1 large clove garlic, crushed
2 hot chili peppers (your choice of heat), diced
1 can diced tomatoes
1 can kidney beans, drained
1 red bell pepper, diced
1 yellow bell pepper, diced
7 1/2 cups vegetable stock
1 pound fresh pumpkin, diced
2 sweet potatoes, peeled and diced
Chili oil to taste (optional)
Fresh parsley for garnish (optional)

Pour the cooking oil into a large pot over medium heat, spreading it out so that it coats the bottom of the pot evenly. Heat the oil for 3 to 5 minutes, then add the onion and sauté it until it is golden-brown in colour.

Stir in the cumin seed, smoked paprika, garlic, and chili peppers, and simmer for 5 to 10 minutes, stirring often. Add the diced tomatoes, kidney beans, and red and yellow peppers, and simmer for 5 minutes, stirring regularly.

Stir the vegetable stock into the pot and bring the liquid to a light rolling boil. Add the pumpkin and sweet potatoes to the liquid, then reduce the temperature to low heat and allow the mixture to simmer until the pumpkin begins to soften (about 30 to 45 minutes). For extra heat, add chili oil to taste.

To serve, spoon the chili onto plates and garnish each serving with a sprig of fresh parsley.

The Spitfire Arms Alehouse
Windsor

Windsor

valley corn chowder with smokey bacon

Makes 6 servings.

- 5 cobs corn, shucked
- 4 slices smokey or maple bacon, chopped into 1/2-inch pieces
- 2 tablespoons butter
- 1 large white onion, finely chopped
- 3 medium potatoes, peeled and cubed into 1/2-inch pieces
- 1/4 cup carrot, peeled and finely grated
- 1 teaspoon salt
- 1 teaspoon black pepper
- 2 tablespoons fresh tarragon, chopped (or 1 tablespoon dried tarragon)
- 3 cups 10% half-and-half cream (blend cream)
- 1/2 tablespoon fresh parsley or chive for garnish (optional)

Cook the corn cobs in boiling, salted water for 10 minutes. Remove the pot from heat, drain, and rinse the corn with cold water to stop cooking. Allow the corn to cool for a few minutes. Slice the corn kernels from the cobs (without going too close to the cobs) and place them in a small bowl. Break the kernels apart from one another with your hands. Set aside.

In a medium-sized skillet, cook the bacon until crisp (about 10 minutes). Place the bacon pieces on a paper towel to drain the grease and set the bacon aside.

Melt the butter in a large saucepan over medium heat. Add the onion and sauté until soft (about 5 minutes), stirring often. Add the potatoes and carrot and fill the pot with just enough water to cover the vegetables. Continue to cook uncovered over medium heat, stirring often, until the potatoes are soft (about 15 minutes). If the liquid level in the pot becomes too low to cook the vegetables, add more water to the pot (just enough to cover the vegetables). When the potatoes are soft, stir in the corn kernels, crisped bacon, salt, pepper, tarragon, and cream. Reduce the heat to low and continue to warm the chowder thoroughly, stirring often to prevent sticking.

To serve, ladle the chowder into bowls and garnish each serving with 1/2 tablespoon fresh parsley or chives.

The End of the Line Pub
Bridgetown

Bridgetown

Annapolis Royal

mains from the land

There are a growing number of Valley chefs and food enthusiasts who are determined to source local meats year-round. Buying locally helps attain economic viability for the agriculture industry, advocates respect for the history and culture of the produce, and enables consumers to live a more sustainable lifestyle. What makes the local food movement in the Valley even more exciting is the global influence that some of the Valley chefs are adding to their local dishes. It is not uncommon to see locally sourced meat influenced by international recipes. Restaurant Le Caveau's Chicken Marrakech is a mouth-watering example of globally inspired local food—chef Jason Lynch sources local free-range chicken from Oulton's Farm in Windsor and jazzes it up with Moroccan spices that give this local dish an international flair.

facing page: Kentville

chicken marrakech

Makes 4 servings.

Marrakech Spice Mixture

3 teaspoons turmeric
1 1/2 teaspoons paprika
1 1/2 teaspoons cumin
1 1/2 teaspoons coriander
1/4 teaspoon cinnamon
1/4 teaspoon cloves
1/4 teaspoon nutmeg
1/4 teaspoon fenugreek
1/4 teaspoon allspice
3/4 teaspoon chili pepper
3/4 teaspoon fresh or dried tarragon
3/4 teaspoon fresh or dried thyme

Place all ingredients in a small bowl and mix thoroughly.

Chicken

1 tablespoon vegetable oil
1 medium carrot, peeled and diced
1 medium Spanish onion, diced
2 stalks celery, diced
1 medium red pepper, diced
1 medium green pepper, diced
3 tablespoons Marrakech spice mixture (see recipe, above)
1 1/2 cups chicken stock
4 chicken breasts (about 5 ounces each), sliced thinly
1/4 cup 35% whipping cream (heavy cream)
1/4 cup cold water
1 tablespoon cornstarch
Salt and pepper to taste
2 cups cooked basmati rice
Sliced local fruit for garnish (optional)

Warm the oil in a large sauté pan on medium heat. Add the carrot, onion, celery, red and green pepper and sauté, stirring often, until the onions are translucent (2 or 3 minutes). Stir in the Marrakech spice mixture and sauté for 30 seconds.

Stir in the chicken stock and increase the heat to high to bring the mixture to a boil. Boil for 2 to 3 minutes. Add the chicken and boil for about 4 minutes, or until cooked through. Once the chicken is cooked, stir in the cream. Reduce the heat to low and allow the contents of the pan to simmer while preparing the cornstarch mixture.

Pour the cold water into a small mixing bowl, then add the cornstarch and stir until the liquid is smooth. Use the cornstarch mixture to thicken the sauce in the chicken pan, stirring the cornstarch mixture into the pan slowly until the liquid in the pan is the consistency of heavy cream. Season the chicken mixture with salt and pepper to taste.

To serve, spoon 1/2 cup basmati rice onto the centre of each plate. Make a bowl shape in the centre of each serving of rice, then pour 1/4 of the chicken mixture into each of the hollowed-out rice bowls. Garnish the plates with sliced local fruit.

Restaurant Le Caveau
Grand Pré

dijon, hazelnut, and parmesan crusted lamb racks with celery root purée

Makes 8 portions.

Wolfville

Lamb Racks

2 tablespoons olive oil, divided
1 1/2 teaspoons chopped fresh thyme (removed from the stem), divided
Pinch ground pepper
1/2 cup hazelnuts, toasted
1/2 cup grated Parmesan cheese
2 tablespoons bread crumbs
3 tablespoons chopped parsley
1/2 cup Dijon mustard
4 lamb racks, cleaned, with trimmings reserved for stock
1 medium carrot, peeled and diced
1 medium white onion, diced
1 stalk celery, diced
4 1/4 cups water
1/2 cup white wine
5 sprigs fresh thyme
2 cups beef or chicken stock
1 teaspoon butter

In a small bowl, mix 1 tablespoon of the olive oil and 1 teaspoon of the chopped thyme with the ground pepper. Spread the oil mixture evenly over the lamb racks and allow them to marinate for 1 to 2 hours.

While the lamb is marinating, place the hazelnuts in a food processor and grate them until finely ground. (Do not over-grate them or they will turn into a paste.) Remove the bowl from the food processor and add the Parmesan cheese, bread crumbs, parsley, and Dijon mustard. Mix them together until they form a very thick paste. If necessary, add water to achieve the desired consistency. Set aside.

Preheat the oven to 450°F. Roast the lamb trimmings in the oven for 20 minutes, or until they have browned and some liquid fat has accumulated. Pour off the excess fat and discard. Toss the carrot, onion, and celery with the trimmings and roast for another 15 minutes. Remove the vegetables and trimmings from the oven and transfer them to a small stockpot.

Add the water, wine, and thyme sprigs to the stockpot. Bring the mixture to a boil and cook it uncovered over medium heat at a steady boil until the liquid has reduced to two cups (about 40 minutes). Strain the liquid off into a heat-proof container and let it stand for 15 minutes.

Skim the congealed fat off the top of the liquid. Pour the liquid into a medium saucepan and stir in the beef or chicken stock. Bring the stock to a boil over medium heat and cook, stirring often, until it has reduced to 3/4 cup of sauce (about 10 to 15 minutes). Reserve the sauce until ready to plate the lamb.

Preheat oven to 450°F. Clean the excess marinade off of the lamb racks. Warm a large frying pan over medium-high heat for 4 to 5 minutes. Pour the remaining tablespoon of olive oil in the hot pan. Place the lamb racks in the pan and sear them for 1 to 2 minutes on all sides, or until they are an even golden brown. Remove the lamb racks from the heat and let them cool for 10 minutes.

Once the lamb has cooled, spread the Parmesan, bread crumb, parsley, and Dijon paste evenly over all faces of the racks. Place the lamb racks in the oven on a sheet tray or cookie sheet and roast for 8 minutes for medium rare or 15 minutes for medium well. Remove the lamb from the oven and let it rest for 5 minutes before serving.

Return the sauce to a boil, then stir in the butter and the remaining 1/2 teaspoon of fresh thyme. Remove the sauce from the heat and set it aside until ready to serve.

Celery Root Purée

1 large celery root, peeled and chopped into 1-inch pieces
1/2 cup 35% whipping cream (heavy cream)
2 tablespoons butter
2 dashes hot pepper sauce
Salt to taste

Boil the chopped celery root in salted water until it is very tender (about 20 minutes). Drain, reserving about 1 cup of the boiling liquid. In a pan large enough to hold the celery root, warm the cream and butter over medium heat. Using a ricer, rice the celery root into the warm cream mixture. (If a ricer is not available, mash the celery root into the cream using a potato masher.) Mix until creamy and smooth. If necessary, thin the mixture with the reserved boiling liquid until it is almost pourable. Season the purée with hot pepper sauce and salt. Cover and let rest about 10 minutes before serving.

To serve the dish, place a mound of the celery root purée in the centre of each of the plates. Tilt the racks of lamb against the purée, and pour the sauce over and around the racks of lamb.

Tempest World Cuisine
Wolfville

farm chicken with nova scotia riesling and chanterelles

Makes 4 servings.

3 tablespoons safflower oil or high-quality canola oil
1 fresh 4-pound chicken, cut into breasts and legs
Salt to taste
Fresh ground pepper to taste
2 shallots, minced
3 tablespoons dark rum
1 cup of Nova Scotia Riesling
3 tablespoons butter, divided
8 ounces (about 2 1/2 cups) chanterelle or baby bella mushrooms, sliced into medium-sized pieces
1/4 cup 35% whipping cream (heavy cream)
1 tablespoon whole wheat or all-purpose flour

Warm the oil in a large cast iron skillet over medium heat. Add the chicken pieces, ensuring that there is enough space between them that they can brown properly without sticking together. Sprinkle the chicken with salt and pepper to taste. Cook for approximately 5 minutes per side.

Add the shallots to the chicken skillet and cook, stirring constantly, for about 1 1/2 minutes. Pour the rum over the chicken and set it aflame with a long barbecue lighter. Flambé the chicken until the alcohol runs out and the flame dies.

Turn the heat down to low and stir in the Riesling. Cover and simmer for approximately 30 minutes, or until the breasts are just cooked. Remove the breasts to a holding plate and simmer the legs for another 10 to 15 minutes, or until the legs are also just cooked. Transfer the chicken legs to the holding plate, retaining the Riesling sauce in the pan. Allow the Riesling sauce to simmer uncovered, stirring often, until it has reduced by half. Set aside.

In a smaller sauté pan, melt 2 tablespoons of the butter over low heat. Add the mushrooms and cook until the juices evaporate (about 10 minutes). Increase the heat to medium and cook for 4 to 5 minutes more, or until the mushrooms are nicely browned. Set aside.

Mix the cream into the Riesling sauce and heat the mixture slowly until steam begins to rise from the surface. While the liquid is warming, place the flour and the remaining tablespoon of butter in a small bowl and work it with your fingers until it is combined (beurre manié). Once the cream mixture is steaming, break the beurre manié into 2 or 3 small pieces and slowly add them to the liquid in the skillet while whisking. Whisk until the butter pieces are fully absorbed and the liquid thickens and appears to have a slight sheen (about 3 to 4 minutes). Place the chicken and the mushrooms into the sauce and gently reheat for 2 to 3 minutes.

To serve, drizzle a tablespoon of the Riesling sauce over each plate. Place a chicken piece on each plate, then pour the remaining sauce evenly over the chicken pieces. Serve with roasted root vegetables or a starch of your choice.

The Garrison House Inn
Annapolis Royal

grilled steak and irish stout pie

Makes 4 to 5 servings.

2 well-marbled grilling steaks (8 ounces each)
1 tablespoon vegetable oil
Salt to taste
Pepper to taste
3 tablespoons olive oil
10 button mushrooms
1 large Spanish onion, cubed
3 stalks celery, cubed
5 cloves garlic, chopped
1 sprig fresh rosemary
4 tablespoons butter
5 tablespoons all-purpose flour
2 cups Irish stout (preferably Guinness)
1–2 cups beef stock
1 tablespoon molasses
1 package puff pastry, pre-made pie dough, or pie dough from your favourite recipe (enough to cover a double-crust pie)
1 egg, beaten

Preheat the barbecue to high heat.

Rub the steaks with the vegetable oil and season them lightly with salt and pepper. Place the steaks on the barbecue and sear them just until they're marked, flipping when necessary to grill them evenly on both sides. Remove the steaks from the heat and place them in a fridge to cool.

Pour the olive oil into a heavy-bottomed saucepan and heat on medium-high. Stir in the mushrooms and onion and sauté until they are a rich golden brown. Add the celery, garlic, rosemary, and butter and stir. Turn down the temperature to medium heat and let the garlic and celery sweat until they are translucent.

Stir the flour into the saucepan slowly, dredging the ingredients until all of the flour is absorbed. Heat for five more minutes, stirring constantly, to cook out the flour.

Pour the Irish stout into the saucepan and cook, scraping the bottom of the pan constantly to deglaze. Add the beef stock a small amount at a time, bringing the mixture to a boil each time the stock is added until the liquid stops thickening and forms a stew-like consistency. Stir in the molasses. Season the stew with salt and pepper to taste and set it aside.

Preheat the oven to 350°F. Remove the chilled steak from the refrigerator and cut it into thin slices. Use the steak slices to line the bottom of a 4-inch-deep casserole dish. Pour the stew mixture over the steak until it reaches just below the lip of dish.

Lay out the puff pastry dough or, if using pie dough, roll out the pie dough so that it is slightly larger than the casserole dish. Cover the dish with the pastry and seal the edges by pinching them against the rim of the dish and trimming off the excess. Use a sharp knife to slice two slits in the top of the pastry to vent steam. Brush the top of the pastry with the beaten egg and sprinkle it with salt and pepper to taste.

Set the pie on the middle rack of the oven, and place an empty pan on the rack below to catch any possible drippings. Bake the pie for about 40 minutes, or until the filling bubbles through the vents and the pastry is golden brown.

To serve, cut the pie into four or five pieces, and place each portion in the centre of a plate. Serve with mashed potatoes and steamed vegetables.

Kings Arms Pub
Kentville

Lakeville

roasted pork ribs in signature spice rub and barbecue sauce

Makes 2 servings.

1/2 cup salt
1/4 cup granulated sugar
2 tablespoons chili powder
2 tablespoons dried thyme
1 1/2 tablespoons ground black pepper
1 tablespoon garlic powder
1 tablespoon onion powder
2 tablespoons dried oregano
2 teaspoons ground cumin
1 1/2 teaspoons cayenne pepper
1 teaspoon cinnamon
2 racks spare or baby back ribs
1 cup Cocoa Pesto's Signature Barbecue Sauce or your favourite prepared barbecue sauce

Preheat the oven to 250°F.

To make the spice rub, combine the salt, sugar, chili powder, thyme, pepper, garlic powder, onion powder, oregano, cumin, cayenne pepper, and cinnamon in a small bowl and mix well.

Vigorously rub the spice mixture evenly over the racks of ribs. Place the ribs in a roasting pan and slow roast, covered, for five hours, or until the meat is tender and falls off the bones when prodded with a fork.

To serve, slice the rib racks in half widthwise and place both halves of each rack on a large plate. Accompany each serving with coleslaw, fresh hand-cut french fries, and a generous helping of barbecue sauce for dipping.

Note: The spice rub can be prepared in advance and stored in an airtight container. It can be used on many types of pork cuts, including pork shoulder, butt, and ribs, using the same cooking directions for all cuts.

Cocoa Pesto Bistro at The Woodshire Inn
Windsor

Windsor

roasted vegetable focaccia sandwiches with sun-dried tomato mayonnaise

Makes 12 servings.

Focaccia Bread

2 cups warm water
2 teaspoons active dry yeast
1 tablespoon sea salt
3 tablespoons olive oil, divided
4 cups unbleached all-purpose flour
2 tablespoons chopped fresh rosemary (or 2 teaspoons dried rosemary)

Pour the warm water in a large bowl, then sprinkle the yeast overtop, taking care not to stir the yeast into the water. Let the yeast sit for 5 minutes. Add the salt, 1 tablespoon of the olive oil, and 2 cups of the flour to the yeast water. Stir until smooth, then add the remaining 2 cups of the flour. Stir the mixture with a large spoon until the dough is smooth and the flour is fully incorporated (about 2 minutes). The dough should be very sticky. Cover the bowl and let the dough rise until it has doubled in volume (about 45 minutes to 1 hour).

Preheat the oven to 500°F. Grease a 13" x 18" baking sheet. Ease the dough onto the middle of the baking sheet using a scraper. With oiled fingers, gently spread the dough into a large oval. Let the dough rest for 5 minutes, then push it out evenly to fill the pan. Drizzle the dough with the remaining 2 tablespoons of olive oil and sprinkle the rosemary overtop.

Place the pan in the oven and immediately reduce the heat to 450°F. Bake until golden brown (about 15 to 20 minutes). Let the focaccia cool in the pan, then cut the bread into 12 equal pieces.

Sun-Dried Tomato Mayonnaise

1/4 cup sun-dried tomatoes, soaked in warm water for 20 minutes
1 clove garlic, peeled
1/4 teaspoon salt
2 tablespoons chopped parsley
1 teaspoon dried oregano
1 cup mayonnaise
1 tablespoon lemon juice

Combine all of the ingredients in a food processor and blend until fairly smooth.

Roasted Vegetables

4 large carrots, peeled and cut into thick strips
1 large red onion, cut into 8 wedges
1 large yellow onion, cut into 8 wedges
2 tablespoons olive oil
1 teaspoon salt
1 bulb garlic, unpeeled
1 bulb fennel, top removed and thinly sliced
1 red pepper, cut into 1/4-inch slices
1 tablespoon balsamic vinegar

Preheat oven to 400°F. Combine the carrots and red and yellow onions in a 13" x 18"baking pan. Drizzle them with the olive oil and

Berwick

sprinkle them with the salt, then toss the vegetables until they are coated.

Cut the top 1/4 inch off of the garlic bulb and wrap the bulb in aluminum foil. Nestle the garlic packet in the centre of the vegetables, then place the pan in the oven. Roast the vegetables, stirring them occasionally, for about 25 minutes, or until they begin to soften and brown.

Remove the pan from the oven and add the fennel and red pepper to the carrot and onion mix. Stir the mixture to coat the fennel and red pepper with oil. Continue to roast the vegetables for another 25 minutes, stirring occasionally so the vegetables around the sides of the pan do not burn. Vegetables should be tender and browned when finished.

Remove the vegetables to a large bowl and set aside. Let the garlic cool separately. Once the garlic bulb is cool enough to handle, squeeze the garlic out of its skin and place the cloves in a small bowl. Mash the garlic, then mix in the balsamic vinegar. Stir the garlic mixture into the vegetables.

To prepare the sandwiches, slice the focaccia pieces horizontally. Spread the inside of each half-slice generously with the sun-dried tomato mayonnaise. Layer the bottom half of each piece with the roasted vegetables, then top with the other half. Serve as is, or grill the sandwiches in a panini press.

Note: For more substantial sandwiches, add mozzarella cheese, pork tenderloin medallions, or grilled chicken breasts.

Union Street Café
Berwick

mains from the sea

The Bay of Fundy boasts the highest tides in the world, which can be seen from the dining rooms of many restaurants on the northwest coast of the Valley. But the bay doesn't just provide diners with spectacular views—it also offers up a bounty of fresh seafood. The harvests from the sea are so fresh that they are caught as the sun comes up and already on your plate by the time the sun goes down. Seasonal Valley vegetables accompanied by sauces made from the best local ingredients are the perfect complement to the catch of the day.

facing page: Halls Harbour

NOVI
YARMOUTH N.S.
11C 772

bacon-wrapped, miso-glazed halibut with carrot-ginger sauce

Makes 4 servings.

4 strips uncooked bacon
4 halibut fillets (5 ounces each)
2 tablespoons miso paste
1/2 cup boiling water
1 tablespoon maple syrup
2 tablespoons fresh thyme
4 cups lukewarm water
1 pound carrots, peeled and chopped
2 tablespoons fresh ginger, peeled and roughly chopped
3 garlic cloves, peeled
1 medium white onion, roughly chopped
Salt to taste
Pepper to taste
4 tablespoons vegetable oil
2 lemons, sliced in half widthwise for garnish (optional)

Wrap a slice of bacon widthwise around each halibut fillet. The bacon should adhere to itself, keeping it in place. Refrigerate the halibut fillets while preparing the glaze and sauce.

To make the glaze, place the miso paste, boiling water, maple syrup, and thyme in a small bowl and mix well. Set aside.

To make the sauce, place the lukewarm water, carrots, ginger, garlic, onion, and salt and pepper to taste in a medium saucepan. Simmer all the ingredients together on medium-high heat for about 25 minutes, or until the vegetables feel very soft when pressed with a fork. Place the cooked vegetables in a blender or food processor and blend until completely smooth.

Preheat the oven to 375°F. Warm the vegetable oil in a large non-stick pan on medium heat. Place the halibut fillets in the oil and sear them for 2 minutes on each side, or until the bacon is slightly cooked. Place the seared halibut fillets on a baking sheet lined with parchment paper and brush them all over with the miso glaze. Bake the fillets for 5 to 7 minutes, or until the outsides are a light golden brown.

To serve, ladle 1/4 cup of the carrot-ginger sauce onto each of four warmed dinner plates. Place a halibut fillet on top of each serving. Garnish each plate with half of a lemon, and serve with an array of your favourite local vegetables.

Old Orchard Inn Resort and Spa
Wolfville

Wolfville

chanterelle mushroom and smoked salmon quiche

Makes 8 to 10 servings.

Crust

1 1/4 cups all-purpose flour
4 tablespoons lard
5 tablespoons unsalted butter
1/4 teaspoon salt
5–6 tablespoons ice water

Place the flour, lard, butter, and salt in a medium-sized mixing bowl. Using your fingers, combine the ingredients until the mixture is coarse and crumbly. Continue mixing, adding small amounts of ice water until the dough clings together. Form the dough into a disc, then cover it and refrigerate it for a minimum of 30 minutes and a maximum of 1 day.

Preheat the oven to 350°F. Roll the chilled dough out on a floured surface to 1/8-inch thickness. Transfer the dough to a pie plate, and trim the edges, leaving a 1/2-inch overhang for fluting. Flute the edges of the dough. Place pie weights on the bottom of the crust and bake it for about 10 to 15 minutes. (If pie weights are not available, spread dried beans or rice over the bottom of the crust in place of the weights.) Remove the weights and bake the crust for another five minutes, or until it is a light golden brown. Set the crust aside.

Filling

2 tablespoons butter
1 pint fresh chanterelle mushrooms
2 egg yolks
2 eggs
1 cup 35% whipping cream (heavy cream)
1 cup milk
2 tablespoons chopped parsley
Salt to taste
Pepper to taste
6 ounces smoked salmon, cut into medium-sized pieces
Pre-baked pie crust (see recipe, left)
1/2 cup cream cheese
Additional fresh chanterelle mushrooms for garnish (optional)

Preheat the oven to 350°F.

Melt the butter in a medium-sized pan on medium-high heat. Add the mushrooms and sauté them until they are tender (about 1 to 2 minutes). Set aside.

Using a whisk, blend the egg yolks, eggs, cream, and milk together in a medium-sized bowl. Stir in the chopped parsley, and season with salt and pepper to taste.

To prepare the quiche, sprinkle the smoked salmon and sautéed chanterelles evenly over the bottom of the pie crust. Crumble the cream cheese into pieces and sprinkle it overtop of the salmon and chanterelles. Pour the egg mixture overtop and bake until the centre is set but not firm (about an hour).

To serve, cut the quiche into 8 or 10 slices and place each slice in the centre of a dinner plate. Garnish with fresh chanterelle mushrooms.

ArtCan Gallery and Café
Canning

Annapolis Royal

eggs maritime

Makes 4 servings.

8 large eggs
1/4 cup butter
1/2 cup 35% whipping cream (heavy cream)
1/2 pound cooked lobster meat, cut into bite-sized pieces
Salt to taste
Pepper to taste
1/4 teaspoon hot pepper sauce (optional)
Greenery for garnish (optional)

Crack the eggs into a medium-sized bowl and beat them well. Set aside.

Melt the butter in a large skillet over medium heat. Add the cream and lobster meat and bring the mixture to a boil, stirring constantly until the cream thickens.

Pour in the beaten eggs, and add salt and pepper to taste. Cook, stirring constantly, for 2 or 3 minutes, or until the liquid is absorbed and the eggs resemble cooked scrambled eggs. If desired, sprinkle the cooked eggs with the hot pepper sauce to add a spicy flavour.

To serve, spoon the eggs onto four plates and garnish each plate with your favourite greenery.

Chez Christophe
Grosses Coques

Clare

golden haddock with saffron-cucumber sauce

Makes 4 servings.

4 haddock fillets (6 ounces each)
1/2 lemon, juice only
Salt to taste
4 tablespoons olive oil
2 tablespoons butter
1 medium white onion, diced
1 large English cucumber, peeled, seeded, and diced
1 tablespoon saffron
3/4 cup fish bouillon
2 tablespoons sour cream
Fresh-ground white pepper to taste

Wash the haddock fillets in water and pat them dry. Sprinkle the lemon juice overtop of the fillets, reserving a dash of the juice for later, and add salt to taste.

Pour the olive oil into a large skillet and warm it on medium heat. Place the haddock fillets in the oil and fry them for 3 minutes on each side, or until they are a golden brown. Set aside.

To make the sauce, melt the butter in a medium-sized saucepan over medium heat. Stir in the onion. Reduce heat to medium-low. Stir in the cucumber and steam, covered, for 3 minutes. Stir in the saffron. Pour in the fish bouillon, stirring constantly and scraping the bottom of the saucepan to deglaze. After 6 minutes of deglazing, stir in the sour cream and cook for 1 minute, taking care not to let the mixture boil. Season the sauce to taste with salt, white pepper, and the remaining dash of lemon juice.

To serve, place the fried haddock fillets on plates and pour the sauce overtop. Serve with rice and vegetables.

Restaurant Composé
Annapolis Royal

Annapolis Royal

lobster risotto with coral butter

Makes 8 servings.

8 small, live female lobsters (about 1 pound each)
1 cup fresh corn kernels
3/4 cup carrots, diced small
1 cup asparagus tips, cut in 1/2-inch pieces
3 tablespoons unsalted butter, divided
1/2 cup white wine
4 cups chicken stock or broth
1 small cooking onion, finely diced
1 shallot, finely diced
2 1/2 cups uncooked Arborio rice (do not substitute other varieties of risotto rice)
Sea salt to taste
Fresh-ground white pepper to taste
2 tablespoons unsalted butter, melted
1/4 cup 35% whipping cream (heavy cream)
3 green onions, finely sliced
8 drops hot pepper sauce
3/4 cup freshly grated Parmesan cheese

Fill a large lobster pot with heavily salted water and bring the water to a boil. Place the lobsters in the boiling water and cook for 2 minutes. Remove the lobsters from the boiling water and place them in a separate lobster pot filled with ice water, allowing them to cool for a few minutes.

While the lobsters are cooling, bring a pot of salted water to a boil. Place the corn kernels, carrots, and asparagus tips in the water and blanch until al dente. Remove the vegetables from the boiling water and place them in a bowl of ice water until cool. Once they have cooled, remove the vegetables from the ice water and set them aside.

Remove the claws from the chilled lobsters and set them aside. Shell the remaining parts of the lobsters, retaining the coral, or roe, for the coral butter (the roe should be raw and dark green, although you can still use it if it has already turned red from cooking). Cut the lobster meat into dice and set it aside.

For the coral butter, place the lobster coral and 2 tablespoons of the butter in a small food processor and blend for about 3 minutes, or until the butter and coral are evenly combined and the mixture is a solid pale green in colour (or pale pink if the roe was red). Set the coral butter aside.

Pour the white wine and chicken stock into a medium-sized saucepan and bring it to a boil on high heat. Once the liquid is boiling, turn off the heat, but leave the saucepan on the burner to keep the stock warm.

Melt the remaining 1 tablespoon of the unsalted butter in a large pot over medium heat. Once the butter has melted, add the onion and shallot to the pot and sauté for 2 minutes, or until the onion and shallot appear slightly shiny and without coloration. Add the uncooked rice and cook for 3 minutes, stirring often. Season to taste with sea salt and fresh-ground white pepper.

Add 1 cup of the warm stock to the rice mixture and stir for 3 minutes, or until the liquid is absorbed. Repeat this step until all of the stock is used. Cook the rice uncovered for 18 minutes, stirring often. When finished, the rice should be cooked but still a bit firm.

While the rice is cooking, preheat the oven to 275°F. Spread the 2 tablespoons of melted unsalted butter evenly over the bottom of a medium-sized baking pan. Spread the lobster claws evenly over the bottom of the pan. Bake the lobster claws for 15 minutes, flipping them once halfway through baking. When cooked, the claws should be firm to the touch. Set the claws aside.

Stir the diced lobster meat, pre-cooked vegetables, coral butter, and cream into the rice mixture and simmer for 2 minutes on low heat. Remove from heat.

Stir in the green onions and hot pepper sauce. Add the grated Parmesan slowly, stirring it in little by little until the rice is creamy but not too watery.

To serve, spoon the risotto into a warm pasta dish and garnish with one of the baked lobster claws. If desired, sprinkle the risotto with Parmesan shavings. Drizzle some of the leftover melted butter from the lobster claw pan over each plate.

Digby Pines Golf Resort and Spa
Digby

maple-glazed salmon

Makes 6 servings.

1 cup maple syrup
1 small white onion, finely chopped
2 tablespoons apple cider vinegar
1 tablespoon Worcestershire sauce
1 teaspoon hot pepper sauce
1 teaspoon salt
1 teaspoon dry mustard
6 salmon fillets (6 ounces each)

Preheat the oven to 450°F.

Combine the maple syrup, onion, apple cider vinegar, Worcestershire sauce, hot pepper sauce, salt, and dry mustard in a medium-sized saucepan. Bring the mixture to a boil over medium heat. Reduce the heat to low and simmer uncovered for 10 minutes, or until the mixture thickens.

Place the salmon fillets into a glass baking dish. Baste the salmon portions generously with 2 tablespoons of the thickened glaze each, retaining the leftover glaze for garnish. Bake for 10 minutes or until the salmon fillets flake easily when pressed with a fork.

To serve, place the salmon fillets on plates and pour the remaining glaze over them. Serve with rice and your favourite seasonal local vegetables.

Pasta Jax Ribs Restaurant
Middleton

Kingston

The Fundy Shore

scallop-stuffed salmon paupiettes with fettuccine in lemongrass cream sauce

Makes 6 servings.

1 (20 ounce) side salmon fillet (10 to 12 inches long), tail end cut off
12 scallops (10/20 count)
Sea salt to taste
Pepper to taste
6 tablespoons olive oil, divided
1/2 cup bread crumbs
1 lemon, juice only
6 stalks lemongrass, chopped roughly
1/2 cup white wine
4 cups 35% whipping cream (heavy cream)
1 1/3 pounds dried fettuccine noodles
1 large Spanish onion, diced small
1 pound dried forest mushrooms, soaked overnight, drained, and roughly chopped or 2 pounds fresh mushrooms of your choice, roughly chopped
4 cloves garlic, finely chopped
4 cups water
24 cherry tomatoes
6 tablespoons chopped parsley

Cut the salmon fillet into 3 long, thin pieces (each about 1/3-inch thick) by using a sharp knife to slice it horizontally from the head end to the tail end. Cut each of these 3 pieces in half widthwise so that you are left with 6 thin slices of salmon. Set the salmon pieces aside at room temperature.

Prepare the filling by seasoning the scallops with sea salt and pepper to taste. Pour 2 tablespoons of the olive oil in a medium-sized pan and warm the oil over medium heat. Place the scallops in the oil and sear them for 2 to 3 minutes, or until they are golden brown (they do not need to be cooked through). Remove the pan from heat and let the scallops cool at room temperature until they are easy to handle. Once the scallops have cooled, chop them into bite-sized pieces. Place the chopped scallops in a medium-sized bowl and mix in the bread crumbs and lemon juice. Stir in sea salt and pepper to taste. Set aside.

Place the salmon pieces on a cutting board so that the head ends are in front of you and the tail ends are farthest away. (To determine which are the head ends, look closely at the grain of the salmon. The grain runs at a 45° angle, and the top of the angle always points to the head end. Also, the tail end should be flatter in thinness and width than the head end.) Use a spoon to scoop the scallop filling into the centres of the pieces of salmon, dividing the filling evenly among the pieces, and leaving 1 1/2 to 2 inches at the head end of each piece of salmon exposed. Roll each piece up from head to tail, taking care not to tear the grain of the salmon. Tie the rolls with butchers' twine so that they do not unravel during cooking. Set aside.

For the sauce, combine the lemongrass, wine, and cream in a small saucepan on medium-high heat, and boil, uncovered, until half of the liquid has evaporated.

While the sauce is reducing, bring a large pot of water to a boil. Add the fettuccine noodles to the pot and cook uncovered on medium heat until al dente. Drain the pasta and set aside.

Heat the remaining olive oil in a large pan, then add the onion, mushrooms, and garlic and sauté them over high heat for 5 to 6 minutes, or until the onion begins to turn almost a nutty colour. Stir in a pinch of sea salt to help take the pungent flavour out of the mushrooms. Pour the reduced lemongrass sauce into the pan and stir. Remove the pan from heat.

While the onion, mushrooms, and garlic are cooking, pour the water in a large saucepan and heat it to 98°F. Gently place the salmon paupiettes in the water and poach, uncovered, for 8 to 10 minutes, turning them halfway through. Remove the paupiettes from the poaching water using a slotted spoon. Cut the butchers' twine from around the paupiettes and discard it.

To serve, place a large helping of pasta onto each plate. Scatter four cherry tomatoes overtop of each serving of the pasta, then place a paupiette on top of each serving. Top everything off with a generous helping of the lemongrass cream sauce, then sprinkle each of the dishes with some of the chopped parsley.

Kellock's Licensed Eatery
Berwick

scallop casserole

Makes 4 servings.

1 tablespoon olive oil
1 tablespoon butter
1/2 small white onion, finely chopped
2 cloves garlic, peeled and crushed
1/4 cup white wine
1 cup 18% table cream (light cream)
1 pound scallops (10/20 count)
1/2 teaspoon salt
1/4 teaspoon pepper
2 teaspoons dried thyme
2 cups cooked basmati rice
1 cup bread crumbs
1 1/2 tablespoons melted butter

Warm the olive oil and unmelted butter over medium heat in a large frying pan, stirring until the butter melts. Stir in the onion and garlic and sauté for about 2 or 3 minutes, or until they start to brown. Stir in the white wine and cook, stirring constantly, until the wine evaporates (about 2 minutes). Mix in the cream, scallops, salt, pepper, and thyme, and bring the liquid to a boil. Allow the mixture to boil for about 3 minutes, or until the scallops are cooked.

When the scallops are cooked, stir in the cooked basmati rice. Warm the rice for 2 minutes over medium heat, stirring often.

Preheat the oven to 350°F. Pour the scallop and rice mixture into an 8-inch square casserole dish. Let it stand for 5 minutes to thicken. While the scallop mixture is standing, place the bread crumbs in a small bowl and add the melted butter. Work the bread crumbs and butter together with your hands until the mixture is crumbly.

Once the scallop mixture has thickened, sprinkle the bread crumbs evenly overtop of it. Bake for 25 to 30 minutes, or until the bread crumbs on top are crispy.

To serve, spoon the casserole onto plates and accompany it with a fresh garden salad.

Boardwalk Café
Digby

Digby

desserts

Whether you are a Sunday baker in the comfort of your own home or a pastry chef in one of Nova Scotia's signature restaurants, the Annapolis Valley has an abundance of fresh seasonal fruit to inspire you. Fresh apples, blueberries, cranberries, peaches, strawberries, and pumpkins can be added to delectable shortcakes, comforting pies, mouth-watering strudels, and a host of other decadent desserts—the perfect ending to a memorable Valley meal.

facing page: Berwick

apple strudel

Makes 16 to 20 servings.

2 1/2 cups all-purpose flour
2 teaspoons white vinegar
4 eggs
6 teaspoons vegetable oil, divided
1 scant cup plus 4 teaspoons water, divided
12 medium unpeeled Red Delicious apples, cored and shredded
1 cup granulated sugar
1 1/8 cup raisins
2 teaspoons strawberry jam

In a large bowl, combine the flour, vinegar, eggs, 4 teaspoons of the oil, and 1 scant cup of the water. Mix until the ingredients are blended together in a sticky dough.

Remove the dough from the bowl and place it on a flat, floured surface. Using your hands, shape the dough into two long rolls (they should each be about 2 feet in length and 2 1/2 to 3 inches in diameter). Brush the dough rolls with the remaining two teaspoons of oil so that they are lightly greased. Cover the oiled dough rolls with tea towels and let them rest for about 15 minutes.

While the dough is resting, stir the shredded apples, sugar, and raisins together in a large bowl. Set aside.

Preheat the oven to 360°F. Once the dough has finished resting, use a rolling pin to flatten each piece out into a long, paper-thin rectangle. Place the dough rectangles on top of large tea towels for easy rolling. Spread the apple mixture evenly over the dough rectangles, then roll the rectangles up lengthwise so you are left with two long, thin rolls that resemble jelly rolls. Brush the outside of the rolls with water to keep them moist.

Place the rolls on a cookie sheet and bake them for about 30 minutes, or until the outer dough has turned a rich golden brown. While the rolls are baking, place the strawberry jam in a small metal mixing bowl in a pan of boiling water. Mix the remaining 4 teaspoons of water into the jam, and stir until the jam is warm (about 3 to 5 minutes). Once the strudels have finished baking, remove them from the oven and immediately brush them with the warm strawberry jam.

To serve, cut the warm strudels into 4-inch pieces and accompany the slices with whip cream or vanilla ice cream.

German Bakery & Garden Café
Annapolis Royal

Annapolis Royal

baked-in strawberry shortcake

Makes 9 servings.

1 1/2 cups all-purpose flour, divided
3/4 cup granulated sugar, divided
2 teaspoons baking powder
1/2 teaspoon salt
1/2 cup milk
1 egg
2 tablespoons melted butter
2 1/2 cups chopped strawberries
1/4 cup butter, softened

In a large mixing bowl, combine 1 cup of the flour and 1/2 cup of the sugar with the baking powder and salt. Add the milk, egg, and melted butter and beat with an electric mixer on low speed for 2 minutes. When finished, the mixture should resemble wet tea biscuit dough.

Preheat the oven to 350°F. Spoon the dough into the bottom of an 8-inch square baking pan and spread the strawberries evenly overtop. Set aside.

In a small bowl, combine the remaining 1/2 cup of the flour and 1/4 cup of the sugar with the softened butter, and mix them together until the contents of the bowl appear crumbly. Sprinkle the flour, sugar, and butter mixture evenly over the strawberries.

Bake for 35 to 40 minutes, or until the top is lightly browned.

Serve warm or cold with a dollop of whipped cream.

Cider Press Café
Berwick

Berwick

The Lookoff

highbush blueberry–lemon delight

Makes 8 large servings.

4–5 cups fresh or frozen Blueberry Acres highbush blueberries or your favourite highbush blueberries
1 3/4 cups granulated sugar, divided
2 eggs
1 teaspoon lemon zest
2 tablespoons lemon juice
1 1/2 teaspoons vanilla extract
3/4 cup melted butter (do not substitute margarine)
1 cup all-purpose flour
1 1/2 teaspoons baking powder
Whipped cream for garnish (optional)
Mint sprigs for garnish (optional)

Preheat the oven to 325°F. Grease a 9-inch square deep-dish baking pan. Pour the blueberries in the pan and spread them evenly over the bottom. Sprinkle 3/4 cup of the sugar evenly over the blueberries. Set aside.

In a large bowl, beat the remaining 1 cup of sugar with the eggs, lemon zest, lemon juice, vanilla extract, and melted butter using a whisk. Mix until well combined. Stir in the flour and baking powder and beat well by hand for about 2 to 4 minutes, or until it forms a smooth batter (do not use an electric mixer).

Pour the mixture evenly over the blueberries in the baking dish. Bake for 45 to 50 minutes, or until set. When finished, it should not jiggle when lightly shaken, and the top should be golden brown. Remove the dish from the oven and allow it to cool for 45 minutes to an hour.

To serve, slice the dessert and place the pieces on small plates. Sprinkle fresh blueberries overtop of each slice, then spoon a dollop of whipped cream on top. Garnish by placing a sprig of mint atop each whipped cream dollop.

Between the Bushes Restaurant
Sheffield Mills

Kingsport

coffee mousse chocolate cake

Makes 12 servings.

Mousse Filling

4 tablespoons very strong brewed Just Us! coffee, cooled
1 package (1 tablespoon) gelatin
2 tablespoons coffee-flavoured liqueur (such as Tia Maria, Kahlúa, or Toussaint)
3 eggs, separated
1/2 scant cup granulated sugar
2/3 cup 35% whipping cream (heavy cream), lightly whipped

Pour the coffee in a small metal mixing bowl, and sprinkle the gelatin overtop, taking care not to stir it in. Leave the gelatin to soften for 5 minutes.

Fill a medium saucepan about a third full with water, then bring the water to a simmer over medium-low heat. Place the mixing bowl over the pot of simmering water, stirring the coffee mixture until the gelatin has dissolved. Remove the bowl from the heat, but leave the saucepan of water to simmer. Stir the coffee-flavoured liqueur into the coffee and gelatin mixture, then set it aside.

In another metal mixing bowl over the simmering water, whisk the egg yolks and sugar together until the mixture is thick enough to leave a ribbon of liquid streaming down when poured from a raised spoon. Remove the bowl from heat and whisk the mixture until it is cool.

In a separate small bowl, beat the egg whites until they are fluffy and white and peaks have formed, then set them aside.

Pour the dissolved gelatin mixture into the egg yolk mixture in a thin stream, stirring it in gently. Chill the mixture in the refrigerator for 3 to 5 minutes, or until it just starts to set. Once the mixture has chilled, fold the whipped cream into the coffee and egg yolk mixture using a spatula, then fold in the whisked egg whites. Set the mousse aside until the cake is ready.

Cake

4 room-temperature eggs
3/4 cup granulated sugar
1 teaspoon vanilla
3/4 cup all-purpose flour
1/4 cup cocoa
1 teaspoon baking powder
1/4 teaspoon salt
Mousse filling (see recipe, left)
Grated chocolate for garnish (optional)
Whipped cream for garnish (optional)
Icing sugar for garnish (optional)
Just Us! coffee beans for garnish (optional)

Preheat the oven to 350°F. Grease the bases of one 8-inch square cake pan and one 8-inch round cake pan, then line the bottoms with parchment paper.

Beat the eggs in a small mixing bowl until they appear thick and lemon-coloured. Add the sugar 1/4 cup at a time, beating well after each addition. Mix in the vanilla. Transfer the mixture to a large bowl.

Mix the flour, cocoa, baking powder, and salt together in a small bowl. Sift 1/3 of the flour mixture over the egg mixture. Using a spatula, gently fold the dry ingredients into the egg mixture. Repeat these steps until all of the flour mixture has been folded into the egg mixture.

Pour 1/3 of the batter into the square pan and the remaining 2/3 of the batter into the round pan. Bake both pans for 10 to 12 minutes, or until toothpicks inserted into the centres of the cakes come out clean.

Allow the cakes to cool for 10 to 15 minutes, or until they are cool to the touch. Once the cakes have cooled, slice the round cake in half horizontally and place the bottom half back in the pan, face up. Trim the edges from the sides of the square cake. After trimming, cut the square cake into 4 equal strips and use these cake strips to line the sides of the round pan (this is the "sponge case").

To prepare the cake, spoon the mousse filling into the sponge case and spread it out evenly. Cover the mousse layer with the top of the round chocolate cake. Freeze the cake for at least 3 hours. Allow the cake to soften in the fridge for 40 minutes before serving.

To serve, decorate the cake with grated chocolate and whipped cream. Garnish with Just Us! Coffee Beans and a dusting of icing sugar.

Note: Use a knife dipped in hot water and wiped dry to cut the cake into slices and serve.

Just Us! Café
Grand Pré

peach-blueberry crumble pie

Makes 6 servings (1 pie).

6 to 8 medium-sized peaches, peeled and sliced
1 cup blueberries
1/2 cup granulated sugar
1 1/4 cups all-purpose flour, divided
1 unbaked 9-inch pie shell (either store-bought or your own recipe)
1/2 cup brown sugar
1/4 teaspoon cinnamon
1/3 cup butter, softened

Preheat the oven to 375°F. In a large bowl, mix together the peaches, blueberries, granulated sugar, and 1/2 cup of the flour. Pour the fruit mixture into the pie shell and spread it evenly. Set the shell aside.

Place the brown sugar, cinnamon, and the remaining 3/4 cup of the flour into a separate medium-sized bowl. Cut in the butter and combine until the mixture appears crumbly. Sprinkle the mixture over the filling in the pie crust.

Bake the pie for 45 minutes, or until the peaches are tender and the topping is golden brown. Remove the pie from the oven and allow it to cool for about 30 minutes.

Serve slices warm with a dollop of whipped cream or a scoop of ice cream.

Evangeline Inn and Motel
Grand Pré

Grand Pré

triple-ginger apple gingerbread

Makes 8 large servings.

1 cup softened butter, divided
3 tablespoons granulated sugar
4 or 5 firm apples, peeled, cored, and sliced thinly (Gravenstein or Cortland are best)
2 1/2 cups all-purpose flour
1 teaspoon ground ginger
1/2 teaspoon ground cloves
1/2 cup brown sugar
1 egg
3/4 cup molasses
3/4 cup hot water
1 1/2 teaspoons baking soda
2 teaspoons fresh grated ginger
2 tablespoons chopped candied ginger

Preheat the oven to 350°F. Line the bottom of a 9-inch round cake pan with parchment paper. Spread 1/4 cup of the butter evenly over the parchment paper on the bottom of the pan. Sprinkle the granulated sugar evenly over the butter. Arrange the apple slices in a fan pattern on the bottom of the cake pan.

Sift the flour, ground ginger, and ground cloves into a medium-sized bowl and mix well. Set aside.

In another medium-sized bowl, cream the remaining 3/4 cup of the butter and the brown sugar together until the mixture is smooth. Mix in the egg and the molasses.

Measure out the hot water in a measuring cup and stir the baking soda into the water. Blend the water and baking soda mixture into the butter and brown sugar mixture. Mix the dry ingredients, the grated ginger, and the candied ginger into the butter and brown sugar mixture and stir until smooth. Pour the batter evenly overtop of the apples in the baking pan.

Bake for 1 1/2 to 2 hours, or until a toothpick inserted into the centre of the gingerbread comes out clean. Allow the gingerbread to cool for 15 to 20 minutes, then turn it upside down onto a plate and peel off the parchment paper. Leave the gingerbread upside-down so that the apple slices are visible.

Serve slices warm with whipped cream.

Leo's Café
Annapolis Royal

Annapolis Royal

Bridgetown

RESTAURANT GUIDE

Acton's Grill & Café on Main Street in Wolfville features local delicacies paired with a selection of fine wines served in an intimate environment. (Cold Raspberry Soup with White Chocolate Mousse and Lemon-Infused Yogourt, page 4)

ArtCan Gallery and Café in Canning offers the perfect combination of fine wine and delicious entrees served in the company of some of Nova Scotia's most impressive local artwork. (Chanterelle Mushroom and Smoked Salmon Quiche, page 45)

Between the Bushes Restaurant in Sheffield Mills, Kings County, is surrounded by sixty acres of highbush blueberries. The restaurant's field-to-fork program sources the freshest seasonal fruits and vegetables and delivers them directly to your plate. (Highbush Blueberry–Lemon Delight, page 71)

Blomidon Inn on Main Street in Wolfville serves leisurely weekend brunches, casual lunches, and candlelight dinners complemented by an award-winning wine list. (Mussels with Double-Smoked Bacon and Vermouth, page 14)

Boardwalk Café on the waterfront in downtown Digby features handwritten daily menus that boast the catch of the day and a variety of fresh homemade dishes. (Scallop Casserole, page 60)

Chez Christophe in Grosses Coques on the breathtaking French Shore specializes in traditional and contemporary home-cooked Acadian cuisine. (Eggs Maritime, page 48)

Cider Press Café in Berwick is a family restaurant featuring a fine selection of homemade soups, sandwiches, salads, and desserts prepared fresh daily. (Baked-In Strawberry Shortcake, page 66)

Cocoa Pesto Bistro at The Woodshire Inn on King Street in Windsor offers unique and exciting dishes showcasing seasonal produce in a historic atmosphere. (Roasted Pork Ribs in Signature Spice Rub and Barbecue Sauce, page 36)

Digby Pines Golf Resort and Spa's renowned executive chef and sommelier, Claude AuCoin, focuses on traditional and international cuisine paired with an extensive array of wines. (Lobster Risotto with Coral Butter, page 52)

The End of the Line Pub is housed in a tastefully restored former Dominion Atlantic Railroad train station on Queen Street in Bridgetown. It serves a selection of traditional pub fare accompanied by more than twenty-five different kinds of beer. (Valley Corn Chowder with Smokey Bacon, page 20)

Evangeline Inn and Motel in the heart of Grand Pré is open for breakfast and lunch, and features a fantastic selection of soups, sandwiches, and the Valley's most sought-after fresh homemade pies. (Peach-Blueberry Crumble Pie, page 74)

Falcourt Inn, situated in a restored fishing lodge overlooking the Nictaux River, offers an extensive menu of gourmet entrees served in a warm, inviting environment. (Ground Beef Soup, page 2)

The Garrison House Inn is located in a restored heritage property across the street from Fort Anne in Annapolis Royal, and features entrees prepared using fresh local and organic foods. (Farm Chicken with Nova Scotia Riesling and Chanterelles, page 30)

German Bakery & Garden Café, located in the Annapolis Royal Historic Gardens, specializes in freshly baked German sweets and breads and offers leisurely lunches in the café. (Apple Strudel, page 65)

Halls Harbour Lobster Pound offers a variety of fresh seafood from the bounty of the Bay of Fundy. Choose your own lobster and enjoy the view of the highest tides in the world from the dining room window. (Lobster Bisque, page 13)

The Ivy Deck Garden Bistro in Wolfville focuses on organically grown market produce cooked with a Mediterranean flare, and serves a variety of vegetarian options. (Chicken Caesar Salad with Sautéed Apples and Cashews, page 7)

Just Us! Café in Grand Pré is one of several Just Us! locations in Nova Scotia, which specialize in serving fair trade coffee and tea alongside light lunches and delectable sweets made fresh in their on-site bakery. (Coffee Mousse Chocolate Cake, page 72)

Kellock's Licensed Eatery in Berwick serves simple but delicious food for breakfast and lunch followed by a dinner menu that will take your palate on a culinary tour of the world. (Scallop-Stuffed Salmon Paupiettes with Fettuccine in Lemongrass Cream Sauce, page 58)

Kings Arms Pub in downtown Kentville features an extensive selection of traditional pub favourites for brunch, lunch, and dinner accompanied by a fine selection of draught beers. (Grilled Steak and Irish Stout Pie, page 33)

Leo's Café in downtown Annapolis Royal is renowned for its fresh-baked breads, muffins, and soups made from scratch. (Triple-Ginger Apple Gingerbread, page 76)

Old Orchard Inn Resort and Spa in Wolfville boasts a breathtaking view of the Bay of Fundy. Its dining room reflects the marriage of land and sea, with fresh offerings from both available daily. (Bacon-Wrapped, Miso-Glazed Halibut with Carrot-Ginger Sauce, page 42)

Pasta Jax Ribs Restaurant on Main Street in the heart of Middleton serves hearty homemade meals made from fresh seasonal ingredients. (Maple-Glazed Salmon, page 55)

The Port Pub and Bistro in Port Williams offers upscale pub fare complemented by a wide variety of beers from their on-site microbrewery. (Porter Cheddar Soup, page 16)

Restaurant Composé is a fine-dining establishment in downtown Annapolis Royal that offers a picturesque view of the Annapolis Basin and specializes in Austrian and traditional Maritime cuisine sourced from local produce. (Golden Haddock with Saffron-Cucumber Sauce, page 51)

Restaurant Le Caveau at the Domaine de Grand Pré Winery in Grand Pré features dishes made from fresh local ingredients that are tailored to accompany the award-winning vintages of the winery. (Chicken Marrakech, page 26)

The Spitfire Arms Alehouse in Windsor serves an amazing selection of ales, lagers, porters, stouts, and seasonal beers, which pair exceptionally well with their internationally inspired pub menu. (Pumpkin Chili, page 18)

Tempest World Cuisine in Wolfville embraces chef Michael Howell's philosophy of buying locally and cooking globally, and offers internationally inspired dishes made up of the freshest local ingredients. (Dijon, Hazelnut, and Parmesan Crusted Lamb Racks with Celery Root Purée, page 28)

The Tin Pan Bakery & Bistro in Port Williams is usually filled with the smell of freshly baked breads and homemade desserts. Proprietor and chef Dee Cook serves a variety of homemade dishes for breakfast and lunch. (Hiibaleipa Rye Bread with Spiced Crabapple Jelly, page 8)

Union Street Café in Berwick offers a welcoming dining room that serves familiar and international tastes, while its cozy sister restaurant, The Wick Pub, offers a great selection of beers and hosts live music regularly. (Roasted Vegetable Focaccia Sandwiches with Sun-Dried Tomato Mayonnaise, page 38)